YARD SALE

ARCHAEOLOGIST!

FROM THE PEN OF DR. PETER J. SHIELD PhD

YOUR GUIDE TO TREASURE HUNTING

IN YOUR OWN BACK

YARD!

Introduction

Fate moves in mysterious ways!

A lifetime of Archaeological research
It was on the tiny Mediterranean island of
Malta, where I had spent 5 wonderful years at
the end of my military career working with the
archaeological Dept. of Cambridge University
on the excavation of Malta's remarkable
Catacombs with Dr. David Trump and the
wonderful Fr. Victor Camilleri.

Victor remained a dear friend for 50 odd years
until his untimely demise on December
15,2011.
During those 5 years I was privileged to
photograph and record all the archaeological
sites on the islands of Malta and Gozo,
including the amazing G'gantija (3,600 – 3,000
B.C.), the earliest freestanding stone
monument built by man.

It predates the pyramids of Egypt and are older than England's Stonehenge. I have spent considerable time at Stonehenge in the 50's and 1988, and most recently with members of my family in 2012.

My work for the then Maltese Government Information Department from 1955 – 1960 also included recording all the treasures left by the Knights and displayed in the museums and Churches on the Islands.

During my two-year return visit to the Island to write my most recent book "Malta –

Mediterranean Jewel", available on Amazon.com.

I was privileged to design a photo marketing program for introduction at all Malta's most frequently visited Archaeological sites. The program was never implemented due to the governments lack of funds. I filmed a pilot program at "Ghar Dalam", the cave of Darkness, for my World of Unexplained Mysteries (Malta) television series which you can watch on YouTube/pjshield (http://youtu.be/T2iQ_jcpZUw)

My work on the remarkable "Shroud of Turin" Mystery resulted in the re mastering of my interviews with the Sturp group, researching the results of their investigative study conducted in 80's into the authenticity of this amazing artifact.

In my 80 odd years I have had the opportunity to work and visit archaeological sites in China, Cyprus, Australia, Central and South America, Ireland, Great Briton, Spain, Japan, Taiwan, and Cambodia, to name but a few.

During the 80's, an Exhibition of my replica artifacts from the Louvre Museum toured Australia and was also used as the basis of my presentation of the Howard Carter Story to Australian High School Students.

For four years I had the privilege to work alongside the amazing Dr. Lonnie Hammargren, ex- Lieutenant Governor of Nevada and a world-renowned Neurosurgeon.

Together we created what I consider to be one of Americas most unusual Antique Mall and treasure market's located in Las Vegas' Boulevard Mall, featuring an exhibition hall dedicated to Dr. Hammargren. I consider it an honor to be the creator of this tribute project to this great Nevadan.

In 2017 the section of the Mall we occupied was rebuilt to house a Marine Exhibit and we were forced to move.

This unfortunately meant the end of our joint exhibition and our Antique Store was forced to move to a smaller location.

The Dr. Lonnie Hammargren Exhibition Hall

If you are not familiar with the Antique Mall concept - let me explain.

Antique dealers and people with large collections of collectable items, such as Dolls, Toy Cars (NASCAR etc.), Stamps, and coins, to name but a few; rent space in an Antique Mall in which to sell their collections.

Because the total transaction is undertaken by the 'Mall', including the collection of any sales tax due, the seller does not need to be present and in most cases, they do not require a Business License or Tax I.D.

For this reason, space in these establishments is much in demand and in my case, Dr. Lonnie

Hammargren and myself waited 7 months for an available booth in one of our local markets.

Finally, in desperation I decided that perhaps we should open our own Mall, and this is of course what we did. "The Hall of Antiquities" in my Magic Kingdom, Pahrump; previously located in the Boulevard Mall in Las Vegas.

The end result is that I have now become what I lovingly refer to as a *"Yard Sale Archaeologist".*

Dr. Peter J. Shield's Magic Kingdom

Pahrump NV

What the heck - you ask - is a Yard Sale Archaeologist?

Well as we developed our Antique Mall, needless to say the first booths to be installed were mine and the good doctors.

After all that is what inspired the project in the first place! Our need to find a suitable location to display and sell some of the unusual pieces that we had collected over many years. And this we did!

It soon became apparent that in my case particularly, what appeared a large collection of artifacts and collectables strewn around my cluttered home barely made a dent in my newly acquired booth. I needed more 'stuff'.

My first resource was my local auction house, where over the last few years of my retirement I had managed to add considerably to my artifacts from around the world, from collectors and deceased estates in the Las Vegas area. In many cases, treasures of great value are sold for pennies on the dollar by relatives who are faced with the unpleasant task of disposing of their deceased loved ones treasured possessions.

Another resource I soon discovered was my local thrift shop (Goodwill, Salvation Army, Savers & Thrift Stores, all of which I shall refer to as 'thrift' stores throughout this work). We ourselves had donated much over the years to these goodwill organizations.

Finally - quite by chance we discovered the 'yard sale'. Referred to as Garage Sales. Boot Sales and Trash and Treasure Markets and of course the "Swap Meet".

You have of course a most valuable tool that 'archaeologists' in my day would have killed for! I speak of course of the internet!

Sites like eBay, and Craig's list are just two outstanding sources of artifacts and collectables.

I suggest you simply type "Yard Sale" into your search engine - this is what I found in Las Vegas.

gsalr.com/garage-sales-las-vegas-nv.html

http://lasvegas.craigslist.org/search/gms

Online auctions should not be ignored, and there are many of them. One that I find great for estimating the approximate value of many of my finds is:

www.invaluable.com

Appropriately named don't you think!

I would like to digress for a moment and explain what prompted me to write this guide in the first place.

Most of my days were spent at the Hall of Antiquities, either working on our "Dr. Lonnie Hammargren Exhibition Hall" or simply pricing and arranging my booths.

Every day I got to meet visitors with a mutual love of Antiques, Antiquities and Collectables. On learning that I am a retired archaeologist, an amazing number disclose not only a love of the archeological profession but a secret desire in many cases stemming from childhood to become the next Indiana Jones!

Though I will always be eternally grateful for the circumstances that brought me into this esteem profession; and I have a world of stories and experiences encountered over my 80 odd years, the life of the average archaeologist falls far short of the image portrayed by Harrison Ford in the ever popular "Indiana Jones" movies.

One of my inspirations and role models was the illustrious Howard Carter who with no archaeological academic credentials spent over 12 years searching the deserts of Egypt before making what is certainly the most famous discovery of all time - The tomb of the boy king Tutankhamen!

Most of my years were spent on my stomach scraping dirt out of the early Christian catacombs on the tiny island of Malta, with members of Cambridge Universities archaeological team and photographing the amazing collections of artifacts that abound on this small Mediterranean Island. If you are interested, you can discover more at http://maltaheritage.com; my web site devoted to these amazing years.

It is my sincere hope that one day circumstances will permit me to return to my beloved island home in retirement for at least 3 months every year.

If you have a true love of archaeology I can think of nowhere in the world where you can see so much of man's history so easily accessible, as the island of Malta.

The following picture and cutting were rescued by one of my darling Granddaughters, to whom I shall be forever grateful.

It shows me (third from the left) at the entrance to St. Agathas Catacombs in 1957.

Born in the Channel Islands and educated in Canada, he left home at the age
of 16 to travel the world. In the early 1950's he became a leading communi-
cations expert with the British Royal Airforce. For five years he was
Associated Press's Photographic correspondent covering the Middle East.
During that time he worked with Cambridge University's Prof. David Trump,
then archeologist to the Maltese Government, on the recording of ancient
artifacts and the excavation of ancient pre-Christian catacombs at Rabat.
During this time Peter was responsible for the illustrations on the Government Tourist Calander and Guide Book. At varying times he has lectured at
Cambridge, Nottingham and Trinity Universities; and to school and church
groups around the world.

So, you wish you had become an archaeologist!

As any dictionary will tell you - you do not need a degree to become an archaeologist! Archaeology is the study of peoples and their cultures by analysis of their artifacts, inscriptions, monuments, etc.

Archaeology developed out of antiquarianism in Europe during the 19th century, and has since become a discipline practiced across the world.

Howard Carter who discovered the tomb of King Tut never attended a university!

Howard Carter

If what you really seek is the thrill of discovery; of finding lost or discarded treasures, I suggest you join my band of "Yard Sale Archaeologists".

All you need is a reliable form of transportation and a good eye for that unique artifact that you are about to discover!

Most 'sales' are held on a Friday, Saturday, and Sunday.

Personally, I select a district and just head out!

Though there is no such thing as a 'bad' district - I find the sort of artifact and collectable I'm looking for in the more exclusive areas of town. Having said that I have discovered some amazing finds in our local Mobil Home parks!!!

This .... as compared to this...........

And by the way I got some great items from them both!

Let's take a look at a couple of items my 'excavations' have unearthed.

I was recently waiting for my son to arrive for a meeting at our local bank. He was delayed in traffic so i decided to walk around the neighboring Salvation Army Thrift store to kill time.

I discovered this very collectable AVON men's aftershave bottle, unopened and in it's original box.

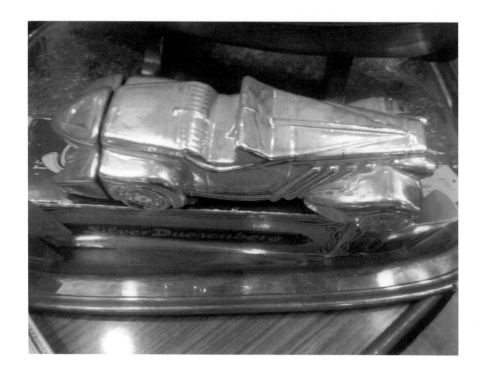

The bottle is in the shape of a Duesenberg car - The asking price $1.25 with tax! It was recently sold to a collector in my store for $25.00!

The old fishing boat and the set of dishes both came from a yard sale. I paid $5.00 for each!

Jewelry boxes $3.00 and telephone $5.00!

Let the Dig begin!

If you are looking for a fun and profitable business, I can highly recommend

becoming a Yard sale Archaeologist.

The procedure is simple:

1. Find a good Antique Mall with available space - be prepared to wait! Good locations are hard to find and in much demand for obvious reasons.

2. If you want to be successful don't buy junk! Look for unique or collectable items that people will want to buy from you!

3. When it comes to collectables - look for names - Marilyn Munroe, Elvis, the Beetles, NASCAR, etc. etc.

4. China and Glass are always popular, but you need to know what to look for. Do your research online!

5. Get out early -Friday morning yields the best buys!

6. Be prepared to 'negotiate! Tell them you are a dealer!

Here are some good examples:

Finally - Follow the signs!

Visit your local Antique Malls for some great ideas!

If you are looking for a profitable part time business that you can start on an extremely limited budget - the Antique and Collectables business is fun exciting and wide open.

Booths are available from around $300.00 per month.

Many Malls have cabinet space from as low as $100.00.

Some charge a small commission (10%) and all charge credit card fees.

Printed in Great Britain
by Amazon

57235177R10022